Music for Double Bass & Piano

BEGINNING TO INTERMEDIATE LEVEL

T0081481

CONTENTS

To access audio visit:
www.halleonard.com/mylibrary
Enter Code
5142-4981-5500-0413

ISBN 978-1-59615-625-8

Music Minus One

EXCLUSIVELY DISTRIBUTED BY

HAL•LEONARD®

7777 W. BLUEMOUND RD. P.O. BOX 13819 MILWAUKEE, WI 53213

TRACK INFORMATION

PERFORMANCE GUIDE
COMMENTARY BY DAVID WALTER

The purpose of this album is to inspire the student to think melodically and rhythmically. Some of these short pieces are gems of melody when played with proper dynamics, vibrato, portamento and rubato; others emphasize rhythm and must be performed with proper accents and staccato at appropriate tempi. Enjoy them!

TURETZKY
Bransle Simple

Drag the first two quarter notes and then allow the eighths to move along. This is *rubato*, in which we give more time to important notes and then steal time from lighter ones. Notice the *tenuto* marks over the quarters. Don't be a "prisoner of the bar line"; rigidity, here, would be boring. Play the opening bar with long bows; then use short, "cute" bowing for the eighths. Imagine the first bar played by trombones, then the eighths by flutes. This will give the piece character and interest.

TURETZKY
Minuet

The Minuet originated as a peasant dance and later became a court dance. Its tempo changed from quick and lively to slow and pompous, a bit of courtly pageantry. This Minuet is in the earlier, lively style: it should have lightness and grace. The sixteenths must be quite short.

TURETZKY
Gavotte

Play this with energy and vigor. Do not confuse "vigorous" with "coarse". Bow strongly and smile!

TURETZKY
Fast Dance

The dots over the notes mean spiccato: short, pointed, dart-like. This will give a happy playful character. Use "natural dynamics": crescendo and decrescendo when the pitches go up and down.

J. S. BACH
Gavotte

Remember that the dots over notes mean "separated" (the Italian word for which is "staccato") and not "short". The dashes over notes mean both "separated" and also "held" (in Italian: "tenuto"). This Gavotte will be elegant if the "dot" notes are *a bit* long and the "dash" notes *quite* long. The slurred groups of two (duplets) will have tiny breath-spaces between them to give a fresh edge to the repeated notes. Each duplet should be played with a small decrescendo for a very soulful "heartbeat" effect.

CATALAN FOLK SONG
The Birds

This piece emphasizes melodic playing. At one time it was traditional for the double bass <u>always</u> to be played with great strength and rhythmic precision. It became a kind of orchestral robot—you know, "Zum, Zum, Zum". Now we understand that it can be played melodiously with very smooth bowing and a singing sound. This simple song is heartbreakingly beautiful when played with appropriate dynamic variety, good sound, vibrato and tasteful portamento. Imitate the human voice. Feel that you are *singing* instead of merely *playing*. This piece was the Pablo Casals "theme song", and was played at the close of each of the Casals Festivals.

IRISH FOLK SONG
My Gentle Harp

Play this sweetly with gentle dynamics, very legato bowing, and quick slides ("portamento"). Sing it before you play it. You will probably recognize it as "Londonderry Air" or "Danny Boy".

TUTHILL
Dorian Minuet

This piece should be played with a variety of tone color and dynamics. For example, the first two sections may be strong the first time and quieter when repeated. In the trio, the ascending quarter-note scale may be very smooth while the second section is staccato and vigorous.

TUTHILL
Allegretto

Contrast the opening eight bars, which should be strong, with the "dolce" bars which follow. The interlude (bars 17 to 24) may be very "loose" in contrast to the "strict" opening.

WALTER
Four Pieces for Double Bass

Each piece has a different "personality". Contrast the different moods suggested in the titles: Lullaby, March, Blues, Dance.

VIVALDI
Sonata No. 4

Until recently many musicians regarded the music of Vivaldi with condescension; Vivaldi was considered a master of "miniatures". Today we respect him as one whose music reached great heights of expressivity, profundity, and passion. This Sonata's first movement is a gem of sweet and thoughtful melody enriched with interesting rhythms and unusual harmonic progressions. It must flow with utmost legato. Bars 9-10, 11-12, 13-14 are examples of "terrace" dynamics: each 2-bar phrase must rise and fall, but each successive phrase must do so at a higher level or "terrace", so that our interest is sustained. Note the cadenza-like freedom of the fourth bar. Starting with an up-bow insures a smoothness and slight crescendo which immediately establishes the gentle character of this movement.

The "echoes" in both movements reflect Vivaldi's fondness for the keyboard instruments of his time, which often had a "soft" and a "loud" keyboard. We must contrast the louds and softs in our "echoes" quite dramatically.

The second movement is a startling contrast to the first: its chief interest is *rhythm,* as opposed to the *melody* of the first; its meter *2* instead of *3;* its dynamics, *powerful and bold* instead of *gentle;* its general character *agitatedly virile* instead of *contemplatively tranquil.* Make all these distinctions: a very noble and beautiful performance will result.

SAINT-SAENS
The Elephant

Zoömusical observation: The elephant is a noble beast. This solo, in his honor, should be played neither hippo-clumsy nor rhino-vicious. It should be played with dignity, solid rhythm and a strong and pleasant sound. Bars 21 through 28, being a caricature of Berlioz' ethereal "Dance of the Sylphs", offer gentle comic contrast and should be played with a slightly saccharine vibrato and a chuckle.

OLD DANCES FOR YOUNG BASSES

Bransle Simple

Anon. 14th Century
Arr. by Bertram Turetzky

4 taps (2 bars)
precede music
Lively (♩ = 156)

Minuet

TELEMANN
Arr. by Bertram Turetzky

3 taps (1 bar)
precede music
Gaîment (♩ = 88)

Gavotte

Anon. 18th Century
Arr. by Bertram Turetzky

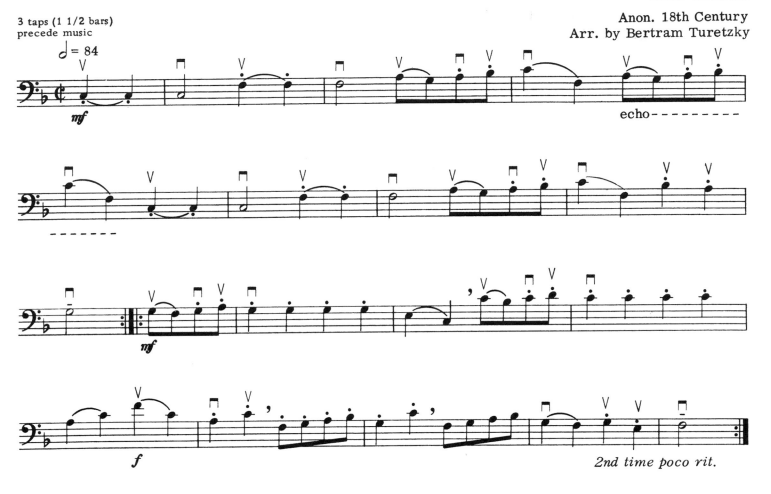

Fast Dance

Track 4 - With Bass
Track 21 - Without Bass

Anon. 18th Century
Arr. by Bertram Turetzky

Gavotte

J. S. BACH
Arr. by Frederick Zimmermann

The Birds

Track 6 - With Bass
Track 23 - Without Bass

Catalan Folk Song
Edited by David Walter

My Gentle Harp

Irish Folk Song
Edited by David Walter

Dorian Minuet

Track 8 - With Bass
Track 25 - Without Bass

BURNET TUTHILL

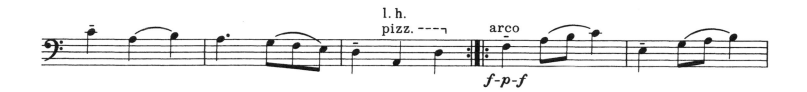

Allegretto

Track 9 - With Bass
Track 26 - Without Bass

BURNET TUTHILL

3 taps (1 bar)
precede music

10

FOUR FOR FOUR

Happy Blues

Track 10 - With Bass
Track 27 - Without Bass

DAVID WALTER

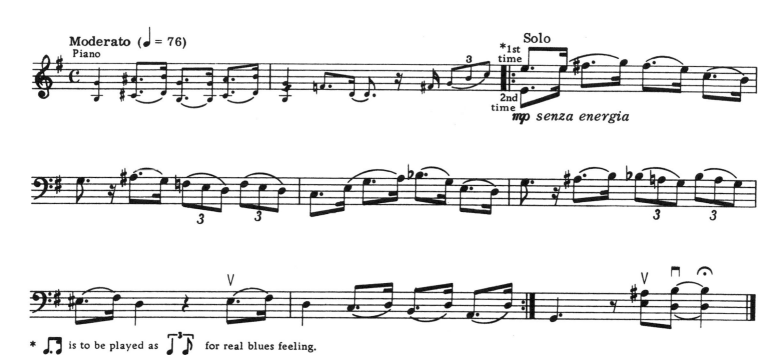

* ♫ is to be played as ♪³♪ for real blues feeling.

Israeli Dance

Track 11 - With Bass
Track 28 - Without Bass

DAVID WALTER

Japanese Lullaby

Track 12 - With Bass
Track 29 - Without Bass

DAVID WALTER

Russian March

Track 13 - With Bass
Track 30 - Without Bass

DAVID WALTER

Sonata No. 4 in B♭

Ist Movement

ANTONIO VIVALDI
Edited by David Walter

2nd Movement

The Elephant

CAMILLE SAINT-SAENS